AF485091

PEACE: YOUR HERITAGE

ALOZIE ISRAEL IKONNE

PEACE: YOUR HERITAGE

Copyright © 1999 by:
Alozie 1. Ikonne
ISBN: 978 - 978-34842 - 0 - 7
Second Edition

Published in Nigeria by:
FOUNTAIN GATE MINISTRIES INC.

For further information or permission write to:
GATE PUBLISHING HOUSE
Imo Concorde Hotel Back Gate
New Owerri
Box 6558 Aladinma P. O.
Owerri, Imo State, Nigeria.
Tel: +234-803-3438251, (0)83-304-931
E-mail: fountainmedia@yahoo.com;
info@fgmin.org
Website: http://www.fgmin.org

Scripture quotations are from the Holy Bible *(King James Version KJV)* except otherwise stated.

DEDICATION

TO THOSE WHO HAVE LABOURED TO
BRING THE PEACE OF THE LORD JESUS
CHRIST TO TROUBLED SOULS.

CONTENTS

PREFACE TO THE SECOND EDITION

God spoke to Jeremiah to write down all He had spoken to him in a book. (Jeremiah 30:2). The point being that books- in whatever shape or volume, contain enormous reservoir of information for personal and collective transformation.

Few books have made such tremendous imprints on the lives of people than this book: **PEACE: YOUR HERITAGE. This book was published in 1999.** I am really amazed that after more than eleven years of publishing this book, there are not much to change in terms of facts and contents. The ideas shared in the first edition have stood the test of time.

The first edition of this book appeared in a format that was both large and unattractive. Despite these obvious shortcomings, thousands are still demanding for this book.

This current edition has been slightly enlarged to accommodate some sections that were not accommodated in the first edition. **Chapter 5 that deals with the issue of confession** has been updated with more Scriptures that teach people how to access peace.

A few minor mistakes on some other chapters have been corrected and the ideas being conveyed made more readable.

It is sincerely hoped that every reader shall gain the same instruction and motivation that has made this book a must for those who desire to have peace, excel in life; and in all spheres of human endeavour.

My sincere prayer is that none shall die at the bank of the River Jordan, when Canaan is just in sight.

Remain a blessing.

Alozie I. Ikonne.

INTRODUCTION

Modern man is at the cross roads today in a world that is fast changing. Technological break-through have brought with them attendant disequilibrium in the social, economic, and environmental spheres.

The natural habit of man has undergone changes brought about by his ingenuity in producing machines and methods that overwhelm his ability to comprehend and handle. There is not only a latent fear, but also equally a real anxiety over the safety of the earth and its inhabitants.

Industrialised nations as well as developing ones are in a mad race to overwhelm each other with weapons of mass-destruction that have the capacity to destroy this earth more than seven times over.

From one corner of the globe to the other, there are stories of wars, famine, earthquakes and disasters of diverse dimensions.

Inequalities in income and ravaging starvation that threaten poorer nations are causes of gloom and despair among the peoples of the world. Rising crime waves and general insecurity of lives and properties have led to general apprehension.

Consequent upon these situations, most people have been driven to suicide bids, and psychiatric conditions. The desire to escape from these "traps" have led more and more people of all ages, into drugs, alcohol, sexual perversion, occult practises etc. These are indeed signs of decaying values and spiritual distortions.

The question that readily comes to the hearts of many people today are: how long will these things remain? What is the implication for man's existence on planet earth? Is there hope for the living?

Within the framework of the present distress, no man can help with an answer as far as human effort is concerned. Nevertheless, there is a bright tomorrow for some people! It is equally possible today for people to have peace and live in peace.

In this volume **PEACE: YOUR HERITAGE**
you will understand the way of peace and
how to posses, experience and live in this
priceless commodity - peace, in a world full of
turmoil.

This book will surely lead you to that peace-
filled-life, wherein you can exclaim, "oh,
there is peace in the midst of all storms".

Enter into the covenant of peace, and enjoy
the heritage of peace this present world
cannot afford. There is a life that is peace-full
and joy-full. When you are connected to this
source of life, you will always have the
resources for replenishment at all times.
With such radiant life, and bubbling joy, you
can then shout like David, in the book of
Psalms:

**Great peace have they which love thy law: and
nothing shall offend them (Psalms 119:165).**

Welcome on board to the path way to peace.
May nothing ever make you afraid to live
from now! The Lord Jesus Christ, the Prince
of Peace blesses you real good.

Alozie I. Ikonne
August 1997

CHAPTER 1
THE FANTASTIC FOUNDATION

Anything that is standing on earth today must have a base, for nothing stands on void platform. God has created the earth on the principle that things stand on other things.

For instance, a man may stand on a table, while the table rests on the ground. When man even attempts to jump, for a few seconds he may be hanging on the air, but he must definitely land on a platform.

In science, when a theory is not based on any empirical evidence, its conclusion is regarded as fallacy - that is, there is no sound basis for proof and assumed result or conclusion. Conversely, if there is existential evidence to postulate, then there is valid ground to conclude.

The Bible clearly and pointedly declares that the foundation of peace is Jesus Christ.

For unto us a child is born, unto us a son is given and the government shall be upon his shoulder: and his name shall be called Wonderful, Counsellor, the Mighty God, the everlasting Father, The prince of peace (Isaiah 9:6)

Jesus truly is the Prince of Peace! For those who may be wondering what the Scripture means, when it declares Jesus to be the "Prince of Peace", here is what the "New Analytical Bible Concordance" defines peace to be: - "Calm repose"

In other words, it means quiet rest, a stress less or serene condition. It is a state of the mind devoid of anxiety and hysteria.

I am aware of the Babel of voices that claim to give peace to their adherents. One doesn't even need to go too far to look for individuals and places that lay such claims.

Where in the world can you find a stress-less, anxiety free and calm environment? The answer simply is that it is not possible in this evil - laden and subversive world.

It is therefore of paramount importance that those who want to have and experience peace must accept the fact that only Jesus Christ has the capability to give genuine peace. The Word of God declares Jesus to be the Prince of Peace. That settles it forever.

In earthly kingdoms, a Prince is an heir - apparent to a throne. He is the most likely person to ascend the throne when the king dies or abdicates his position. If peace means calm repose, then absence of peace means fear and anxiety.

Just as Jesus is the prince of peace, the Devil is the prince of fear and anxiety. It is therefore logical that one cannot be in the camp of Satan and expect to be full of peace. A man can only offer what he has.

TWO PARALLELS

The origin of evil is what seems inexplicable to most people. Some have questioned the wisdom of God in creating the earth, and allowing a wicked creature like Satan to stay around, mess things up, and attack every attempt of man to enjoy the earth the Lord has made.

Without going into the intricacies of how the Devil came to the earth and spoiled things, let us accept the truth of the Word of God that there is an adversary of man in the person of a being called Lucifer, who later became the Devil because of his evil ways.

Be sober, be vigilant; because your adversary the devil, as a roaring lion, walketh about, seeking whom he may devour. (1 Peter 5:8)

The basic ministry or work of the Devil is to kill, steal and to destroy (John 10:10). The Devil is a wicked foe of man whose modus oparandi is deceiving his victims, and later enslaving them to rebel against God, and reject God's good intentions.

When these victims are in disobedience to God, they are never happy. Most times, they are in fear, anxiety, and under all forms of mental and emotional torture.

The Devil keeps them like a trained prison guard so that they do not escape his grips. They indeed have no freedom and rest. Such lives are really miserable, vexed and unfulfilled.

Such a life that has been trapped by Satan is denied the abundant life and is continuously bruised and battered on all sides.

...Is this the man that made the earth to tremble, that did shake kingdoms; That made the world as a wilderness, and destroyed the cities thereof; that opened not the house of his prisoners?
(Isaiah 14: 16-17)

As many as have accepted his lies and deceit (remember he is the Father of lies), he keeps in bondage to various vices - adultery, drunkenness, occultism, drug addiction, strife, envy, murder, violent robberies and all manner of depravities men have fallen into these days.

In God's original intention, man was created in the image and likeness of God. Man has the innate ability to understand between good and bad, virtue and vice etc. Man has God's basic characteristics - will, emotion, and conscience.

And God said, let us make man in our image after our likeness: and let them have dominion over the fish of the sea, and over the fowl of the air, and over the cattle, and over all the earth, and over every creeping thing that creepeth upon the earth. (Genesis 1:26)

It is the image of God in man that the Devil has succeeded in distorting.

The cumulative effect of working outside of God's good intentions is what now causes man to live in fear, worry and anxiety over his life and destiny.

And the Lord called unto Adam, and said unto him, where art thou? And he said, I heard thy voice in the garden, and I was afraid, because I was naked, and I hid myself. And He said, who told thee that thou wast naked? Has thou eaten of the tree, whereof I commanded thee that thou shouldest not eat? (Genesis 3:9-11)

Adam's hiding ministry had its origin from the violation of God's moral laws. Like Macbeth who murdered sleep, there is no hiding place for people who are living in rebellion to the laws of God. All rebels hide from God.

Those people who have even built earthly palaces, discover to their dismay that comfort does not come from the reward of iniquity.

There is no peace, saith the Lord, unto the wicked. (Isaiah 48:22)

From city to city, and from country to country, there are evidences of shattered lives and disillusioned people.

There are many tormented, hopeless and helpless thousands who are victims of the Devil in varying degrees.

A careful observation shows that there is a foundation of curses, pain and fear which the Devil laid for those who will obey his voice, which they that follow, find themselves in the very pit of darkness.

JESUS' FOUNDATION

The Bible says that Jesus Christ is the Prince of Peace. The implication of this statement is that before the arrival of Jesus to this earth, there was already a **prince** whose specialty was in masterminding wars, murders and general upheaval.

It is the devil that instigates national leaders to wage wars against other nations. This prince of darkness is responsible for divorce, rebellion of children against parents, economic dislocation among families etc.

Nothing stopped the Devil except occasional divine intervention by God through the ministry of angels and specially anointed men who God used to advance His cause.

The works of the Devil that originated from the foundation of evil were the main reasons why God manifested Jesus Christ.

He that committeth sin is of the devil, for the devil sinneth from the beginning. For this purpose the Son of God was manifested, that he might destroy the works of the devil (1 John 3:8)

At the time Jesus was born, there was general fear and insecurity, arising from the activities of the occupying Roman forces. That was why John the Baptist chided the soldiers not to engage in extortion when they came to him for baptism (Luke3: 10-14).

The shepherds that witnessed the first birthday announcement of Christ by the angels were told why Jesus was born and what He has come to do on earth.

And there were in the same country shepherds abiding in the field, keeping watch over their flock by night. And, lo, the angel of the Lord came upon them, and the glory of the Lord shone round about them; and they were sore afraid. And the angel said unto them, fear not: for behold I bring you good tidings of great joy, which shall be to all people. For unto you is born this day in the city of David a saviour, which is Christ the Lord.... And suddenly there was with the angel a multitude of the heavenly host praising God,

and saying Glory to God in the highest, and on earth peace, good will toward men (Luke 2:8-11, 13-14)

Look at what the angel of the Lord said to those troubled and trembling hearts: *fear not*! It is difficult to keep rejoicing while fear reigns.

That is why throughout the Scriptures, before God gives any man a miracle, He deals with the person's fears first. God is aware of the fact that when fear goes away, faith begins.

The foundation of Jesus' Ministry on earth is re-establishing the peace of God in the hearts of men. His ministry from the very beginning was clear: **establish the peace of God upon the earth.**

Across the nations and continents, men are holding Peace Conferences and even giving prizes to those who have been adjudged to contribute to world peace.

If every leader will acknowledge that without Christ, nations and kingdoms will be in crisis, they would have stopped procuring peace by human efforts.

Pause for a time, and ask yourself this question: why is it impossible for world leaders to achieve global peace in spite of peace conferences that have been held since the 1930's?

Why is there no real peace in the Middle East today, despite claims by world peace experts to find meeting grounds for reconciliation? The answer is simple: **The Prince of Peace Himself is not part of the peace process**, and so it is bound to fail.

Dear reader, do you need peace in your life? Do you want your home to be filled with the peace of God? Then let me point you straight to the source of all peace.

Throw away every method, system or religion that promises you peace of God outside of Jesus Christ.

When you invite the Prince of Peace, He will come in the full strength of His power, and will replace the devilish foundation that has put you into the peace less condition you have found yourself, with the Jesus foundation of joy and peace.

Thou will keep him in perfect peace, whose mind is stayed on thee: because he trusted in thee.
 (Isaiah 26:3)

There is a firm promise of keeping in perfect peace those whose hearts are set on Him. Has your heart been set on Him? Are you secretly thinking that you still have an alternative in this world apart from Jesus Christ?

Put aside such thoughts, and admit finally that nothing can guarantee you peace, outside of the knowledge of the Prince of Peace Himself- Jesus Christ of Nazareth!

O that thou hadst hearkened to my commandments! Then had thy peace been as a river, and thy righteousness as the waves of the sea.
(Isaiah 48:18)

The Prophet of God Isaiah connects obedience to 'His commandments' to the route to a life of peace. All through the Bible, the delivery of His blessings is tied to specific obedience to specific instructions.

Deliberate decision to honour His Words at all times has always been the route to stay established on the face of the earth.

No one that ever ignores His commands has a future in His covenants with His people.

Be encouraged in your pursuit of His will. No matter what the enemy says to you, hold on to His promises. God has never failed, and will never fail. Let His peace come upon you right now.

It is possible. It is your right and privilege to dwell in peace. Receive His Words like a child. Expect His peace upon your life now, in Jesus name!

CHAPTER 2

FINDING YOUR BEARING

What then? Are we better than they? No, in no wise: for we have before proved both Jews and Gentiles, that they are all under sin; As it is written, there is none righteous, no, not one. There is none that understandeth, there is none that seeketh after God....Their throat is an open sepulchre; with their tongues they have used deceit: the poison of alps is under their lips: Whose mouth is full of cursing and bitterness; Their feet are swift to shed blood: Destruction and misery are in their ways: And the way of peace have they not known (Romans 3:9-17).

The year 1979 will remain evergreen in the minds of historians and Bible scholars. It was a year when there was a handshake across the desert.

Two sworn-enemy nations: Egypt and Israel signed the historic Camp David Accord, (CDA) that formerly ended official hostilities, between two nations whose history of enmity has spanned over 3000 years.

The accord brokered by the USA, under former President Jimmy Carter, brought together the then leaders of Egypt and Israel - Anwar Saddat and Menachin Begin respectively, to sign a Treaty Of Friendship.

For Egypt and Israel, they have found at least, a way to peace, which has greatly reduced the tension in the Middle East. However, for millions of people across the world, the search for peace in the midst of heightening tensions has been unfruitful.

Some will pay great ransoms to secure peace for their houses, families, towns and countries. Concerned leaders in the industrialised/militarised countries have been holding conferences to find *ways* and *means* of securing world peace.

In the last twenty years, the United States, and the (then) USSR, led by the Russian Federation have held Strategic Arms Limitation Treaty (SALT) Conventions. Actually they have signed SALT 1 & SALT 2 Treaties.

In the recent past, they have added the START (Strategic Arms Reduction Treaty) conventions. The military powers of the world have realised that mere possession of strategic weapons does not guarantee the owners immunity against possible aggression from enemy states.

The under guiding principle for these conventions is aimed at reducing the stockpile of nuclear warheads that are threatening the peace of the world. The question then is: how far have these efforts gone in allaying the fears of nations on possible nuclear holocaust? The answer simply is that these efforts have not really proved effective in maintaining world peace.

Peace is not located in this world. Jesus pointedly told his listeners that in this world, they should expect tribulation (John 16:33), but added also the good news to His followers: **be of good cheer, for I have overcome the world**.

The gospel of our Lord Jesus Christ is all about peace to those who receive it.

How beautiful upon the mountains are the feet of him that bringeth good tidings, that publisheth peace; that bringeth good tidings of good, that publisheth salvation; that saith unto Zion, thy God reigneth! (Isaiah 52:7)

The gospel is the carrier of peace. It is the only force that binds up the broken hearted sets the captive free and liberates every form of satanic shackles around the lives of people.

When Jesus began His public Ministry, the first thing He announced as His agenda was the issue of peace in the lives of people. When a person is bound in any way by the powers of Satan, the peace of that soul cannot be guaranteed.

Poverty, frustration and stagnancy are forces that can induce a person to live in anxiety and fear. To destroy the works of the Devil and to enthrone the will of God in the lives of people is the purpose of the gospel.

The spirit of the Lord is upon me, because he hath anointed me to preach the gospel to the poor; he hath sent me to heal the broken hearted, to preach deliverance to the captives, and recovery of sight to the blind, to set at liberty them that are bruised. (Luke 4:18)

Many people are in chains. More are in webs of confusion and anarchy the Devil has wound around them. Some people have discovered the power of the gospel and have accordingly received Jesus into their lives, at the same time, so many are ignorant and are wallowing in self-pity, not knowing how to escape the traps of the enemy.

Recently, I was sharing with a man who was obviously treading on the "rough side" of life. To my amazement, this man does not believe in total commitment to the Lordship of Jesus Christ. To him, being **fanatical** about serving Jesus is an exercise for those who are not serious minded.

Like that man, many people have not realised that the most potent force in transforming any life today on earth is the gospel of our Lord Jesus Christ. Those who have been shackled by many forces of evil are those who have locked their hearts against the voice of God.

The primary ministry of Jesus Christ is to deal with these forces - poverty, healing to the hurting, deliverance from satanic bondage, restoration of sight (both physical and spiritual eyes), and liberty to those who are bruised. He declared He has come to set the "captives free".

Every other event and circumstance in the lives of people who are searching for peace is summarised in this word: **captivity**.

All those whose peace has taken a flight are in captivity. They need to be rescued.

A principle for re-discovery is that every restoration begins at the point of departure. When a man intends to go to point A, and finds he is going on point B, he has to go back to the road junction in other to re-connect to the right route. Men and women have rebelled against the Laws of God.

Every broken law has appropriate sanctions against offenders. God's judgment is that all men have sinned and fallen short of the glory of God (Romans 3:23). It is therefore the gospel that points man back to God - the source of peace.

Remember that God is a spirit. The Bible equally says that one of the fruit of the spirit (regenerated human spirit) is peace.

But the fruit of the spirit is love, joy, peace, long suffering, gentleness, goodness, faith....
(Galatians 5:22)

We need to be connected to the Spirit of God so that peace - a fruit of the regenerated human spirit will flow into our hearts. The degree of connection determines the flow.

That is why it is impossible for anyone who is not genuinely born-again by the Spirit of God to enjoy lasting peace.

It is unfortunate that some people have tried to find peace in the pursuit of money, alcohol, drugs, gambling, sports, sex, etc. Experience has shown that those ways of running away from the realities of unregenerate life have not helped people.

Sometime ago, we received the testimony of a man who had been unable to sleep for some months. Medical diagnosis said he was suffering from insomnia. He lost his peace and had been thinking about the numerous things that had gone bad in his life.

He even stopped attending his denominational Church for a very long time. He had given up hope on life and was just waiting for the worst, until someone directed him to our gospel services.

After listening to the Word of God, he came back two days later to testify how the gospel was able to give him peace, which caused his sleepless nights to disappear. Today that man is one of the enthusiastic fellows around town.

Right now he has even joined in the ministry of encouraging others to hold on to God.

It is vain for you to rise up early, to sit up late, to eat the bread of sorrows: for so he giveth his beloved sleep. (Psalms 127:2)

There is a firm promise that the Lord gives His beloved sleep. Are you beloved of the Lord? The Lord is the way to peace. Find Him today and expect great peace to flood your heart.

He is waiting to pour enough doses of peace into your sorrowful heart. You are not meant for sorrow imposed by the Devil. God wants to restore your life with joy abundant from Jesus.

When the Disciples of Jesus were troubled by a storm on a lake they shouted like most troubled persons would react. Jesus got up, rebuked the storm and the wind, and commanded it to have peace and there was a great calm!

And he arose, and rebuked the wind, and said unto the sea, peace be still. And the wind ceased, and there was a great calm. (Mark 4:39)

He is right now ready to give the right command to your case, and I can assure you in the name of Jesus Christ that all your storms will cease. Will you turn your troubles over to Him?

CHAPTER 3

RENEWING THE MIND

There are keys that determine behavioural patterns in life. For most people, what they were, who they are, and where they are going, can easily be found as one interacts with them.

One outstanding fact that has emerged today among those who study human behaviour(s) is that most people are at cross roads about the issues of life.

The pressures of living in a changing world have brought a lot of people to emotional confusion. Anywhere you see any of life's uninvited guests, the exclamation has always been: why me? What have I done to deserve these? That many people are confused and hurting is a fact of life. But how people handle their problems is a function of their inner make-up.

That is why one calamity can set some people on the downward slide for life. On the other hand, some others grapple with problems and turn-around bad situations into opportunities for victory and celebration.

Many have questioned the idea of a loving God in the midst of suffering and hardship. Some have equally suspected the intentions of well-meaning friends and associates during periods of crisis and grief.

However, the difference between those who quickly resort to suicide, and those who pass through hardship to the side of freedom, lies in their mind condition, which definitely results to their conduct.

There are people who have been toughened by poverty; there are those who have suffered either the loss of a husband/wife, children, friend, etc. There are equally those who have undergone the trauma of divorce and separation.

In all these situations, what makes a man stand or fall in "the day of adversity" is his faith or lack of faith in God. Those who have faith in God can, like the David of old call upon God in the day of trouble and have an answer.

And call upon me in the day of trouble: I will deliver thee, and thou shalt glorify me. (Psalms 50:15)

In over a decade of counselling with believers and unbelievers alike, I have noticed one consistent pattern among those who have resorted to taking matters into their hands. Most people insist that they have been cheated or that their rights have been denied them.

I have often applied the principle of objective (dispassionate) analysis of the conditions, and the results in most cases have been that people often acted based on insufficient information or outright ignorance. When such people know the facts of their cases, some have always laid down their arms and sought for peace.

I remember a sad incident I was privileged to see some years ago. There was a care - free man, while the wife was the detailed and meticulous type. Their marriage of over twenty years started developing cracks. With increasing time they became more and more alienated from each other.

One day this woman told me all the atrocities the husband had committed. In fact, her story can fill a whole trailer load, if it were to be converted to goods. Friends and relatives had mediated between the two, but the woman still held on to her position. Every day, she would recoil to her shell, and kept on worrying and pitying herself about a failed relationship.

It became a serious situation when she interpreted her self-worth and value through her matrimonial circumstances. Whoever had the chance of visiting her would be inundated with the latest misbehaviour of her husband. Any attempt to make her see the positive side of her husband was fiercely resisted. She insisted the man had to accept all blames and atone for all his foolish behaviours.

I was privileged to observe the man's way of life from afar, and discovered that the man was that kind of care-free and jolly good fellow who was willing to make amends, except that the wife did not see the possibility of their ever reconciling.

I persuaded the lady to change her attitude towards the man, but she was too made-up for any alteration of the status quo. She began to carry her burdens to the extent that she developed insomnia (sleepless nights).

Increasingly, she became withdrawn and suffered all manner of cramps. She developed full arthritis and manifested signs of suicidal tendencies. The rest is now history as the woman ended up in an inglorious way - she committed suicide.

The question then is: why is it not possible to avert certain man-induced pains and sorrows when God is willing to change situations for good? Now open your Bible with me let us search for the secret of lasting deliverance from the power of restlessness and anxiety.

I beseech you therefore, brethren, by the mercies of God, that ye present your bodies a living sacrifice, holy, acceptable unto God, which is your reasonable service. And be not conformed to this world: but be ye transformed by the renewing of your mind, that ye may prove what is that good, and acceptable, and perfect, will of God. (Romans 12:1-2)

Paul the writer of the Book of Romans says, "I beseech you". He is just saying, I plead with you. Having considered how rich and vast the grace of God is, he implores us to avail ourselves of the provisions of God's mercies.

The mercy of God is the carrier of God's miracle touch. We can contact this mercy by abandoning our lives at God's care and love.

As we consider what this mercy can do for us, we will discover to our amazement that our minds will be renewed. That is to say, there will be re-invigoration of the power of the mind to know what is good, acceptable and ultimately, the perfect plan (will) of God at any particular instance.

Friend, the card is laid bare before you. You choose between renewing your mind or staying on the old land of your reasoning and reaping the consequences of prolonged depression. The greatest enemy of change is a mind- set that has been held hostage by the wrong information.

Paul says that the way of knowing the good, acceptable and perfect will of God is progressively tied to renewing the mind. You may be asking what the renewal of the mind is. It is simply replacing old thought processes and ideas with new and often more enlightened thought and ideas, in order to move forward.

Every restoration begins at the point of departure. The point of departure is where one missed out of the original thing or plan. It is at the point where one's boat of comfort began to leak while on the sea of pleasure.

In most cases, mistakes occur when people derail from the standard of the Word of God and give in to self-serving schemes that (in most cases) are the causes of anxiety and fear. (Please see my book: ***How To Build With Nothing;*** chapters 1 and 2).

Only fresh inflow of ideas and insight from the Word of God can turn the captivity of the soul around. The inability to renew the mind has caused many professing Christians spiritual drain - pipes. Miracles are gained and lost almost at the same rate because of laziness to study.

The worst captivity on earth is the enslavement of the soul by the wrong idea. It is the Word of God that gives fresh insight and understanding to people.

The entrance of thy words giveth light; it giveth understanding unto the simple. Thy testimonies have I taken as an heritage for ever: for they are the rejoicing of my heart. (Psalms 119:130; 111)

When a believer makes the study of the Word of God his or her desire every fog and cloud of uncertainty dissolve.

I remember counselling with a man who seemed to be the most pessimistic fellow I have ever seen. Everything around him was bad and even the promises of God are for a special few. This spirit of pessimism affected this man's world-view.

He was often depressed and could neither see well in people or the world. I had to take him through a process of "intellectual flush out". By the time we were through, he was able to reject those negative views and beliefs that were the platforms upon which the Devil tormented his life. Today, that man is one of the most vibrant fellows around.

A renewed mind is a renewed life. When a person is beclouded with the uncertainties of life, there is a loss of bearing (touch) with the source of life. The result obviously is that people resort to medical check-up, without going for Jesus check-up.

In Paul's letter to Timothy, he released the key for mind renewal.

Study to show thyself, approved unto God, a work man that needeth not to be ashamed, rightly dividing the word of truth. (2 Timothy 2:15)

The key word here is `study'. Paul is simply saying, receive enlightenment to assess yourself whether you stand approved by God or not.

Now are you cast down? May be you have been hurt and you are seeking for revenge? Or your mind is simply made-up never to forgive your adversary? It may be that you have been unfairly treated and you feel that there is no need staying peaceful, or even living any longer. It is not always easy to ignore hurts and ill-treatments. But one could always change prevailing circumstances if the God angle is introduced.

Cheer up friend, God has said in His Word, "vengeance is mine and I will repay"(Romans 12:19). If through the education of your mind, you know what the Word says, you will be willing to allow God solve your problems than taking laws into your hand.

Those who resort to self-help discover at last that they did not really have the final solution.

He is wise in heart, and mighty in strength: who hath hardened himself against him, and hath prospered? (Job 9:4)

A major truth I have personally discovered for myself is that God is all-knowing and all-wise. No one can resist God without being resisted. When God enforces resistance, the fellow is bound to slow-down or is out rightly halted.

Paul not just charged Timothy to study, but also to "show himself approved". What Paul is simply saying is, study to manifest yourself as a workman!

Oh how many multitudes have forgotten that they are workmen for God? When a man is given a work to do if he is honest and trustworthy he labours and at times puts in extra hours to finish his work.

 The best way to gain God's approval is in studying His Word, and obeying the commandments, injunctions and statues. Knowledge gained in study produces a renewed mind, and a renewed mind begets a change in thought - pattern. A change in thinking produces a new personality that ultimately gives rise to new attitudes and behaviours.

Today, there are multiplied thousands who want to sing "the Lord's song" in a strange land. Their views and opinions about things are informed either by insufficient knowledge or outright ignorance of what the Word of God says. Like, Apolos who was preaching John's Baptism in an era of Christ's resurrection before he was corrected (See Acts 18:24-28).

They want the Word of God to work for them, but where they stand makes it difficult for God to help them. Friend, do you know that what you believe can either make you receive from God, or resist His hand of blessing and favour?

Some time ago, a young man came to my office for counselling. I discovered that he needed assistance over demonic attacks. On closer enquiry, I was shocked to discover that he believed those attacks had to be there in order to force him to engage in "spiritual warfare".

In other words, if the attacks do not come, he may not be able to pray effectively. This young man is not alone in this satanic trap. Nowhere in the Word of God is it written, "That the Devil will help us to pray better".

Another instance is the issue of poverty and wealth. I have seen Preachers who with all their being argued that prosperity is evil, and that Jesus Christ lived a poor life.

The truth is that Jesus lived a modest life. There is no way a poor man can maintain a pastoral Ministry of more than twelve full-time Pastors. Jesus never begged anyone for alms. He lived an abundant life, and became a blessing to those in need.

Poverty in all its ramifications is a curse. The Scriptures told us that Jesus became a curse for us in all things. His so-called poverty was to deliver us from the curse of poverty. In a sense, His **poverty was a substitution one.**

For ye know the grace of our Lord Jesus Christ, that, though he was rich, yet for your sakes, he became poor, that ye through his poverty might be rich. (2nd Corinthians 8-9)

The bottom line of Jesus' poverty is that "we might be rich". This is the will of God. We ought to be rich in all aspects of our Christian life - health, food, holiness, righteousness, integrity etc.

Some people feel that poverty breeds more holiness (this is unscriptural). I'm yet to find a portion of the Scriptures, which support this assertion.

If you consider those who pilfer offering money, quarrel and fight over N500 (five hundred Naira), it is mostly those who are poor - poor in the knowledge of the Word of God, poor in their commitment to the cause of the kingdom of God; poor in giving etc. Unless they change their hearts, they stand the risk of missing the kingdom of heaven entirely.

Over comers in this present world are those whose minds have been renewed after the rudiments of the Word of God. There is an urgent need for God's people to go back and search the Scriptures. Throw away those ideas and practices, which though may be normal, but may not be right.

Renew your mind and renew your strength, this is the way to escape the corruptions that are in this present world through lust.

But whoso looketh into the perfect law of liberty and continueth therein, he being not a forgetful hearer, but a doer of the work, this man shall be blessed in his deed. (James 1:25)

The Scripture says, "Whoso looketh". That is whoever looks into the Bible with the intention of finding something of benefit to him or her shall be blessed in that endeavour.

Some people have been searching for the secret of peace and tranquillity to no avail. God's Word contains all the answers to life's perplexities. From the Word, one can discover the secret of lasting deliverance from fear and anxiety, which is renewing the mind every day with the Word of the Living God.

THE POWER OF FOCUS

As we are concluding this chapter, may I remind us to remember one key that enables over comers to receive miracles.
Many people think that reading the Bible guarantees instant changes. The Word of God changes things though. But definite changes come only to those who have a **staying power**.

Our text above in James chapter one talks of those who 'continue therein'. Ability to remain focussed on the Word of God will deliver the good things of life to those who constantly speak the Word of God in their situation, no matter the facts on the ground.

Commitment to reason and share in the Word of God consistently would lead to unspeakable changes. God created all things through the Word and has also wrapped all things within the Word.

Therefore, anyone who looks at the Word daily for information and direction shall begin to fly higher in the realm of the spirit. In addition, insight will be granted on burning issues to anyone who watches over the Scriptures.

Do you want to live? Then look at the Bible. The beauty of your entire life is tied to your daily focus on the Word. This is because every person becomes what he or she beholds.

When Moses went to the mountain to receive the Ten Commandments, he stayed so close to God that by the time he came back to the camp of Israel, his face was shining like that of an angel. The radiance was so glorious that the children of Israel begged him to cover his face.

The chameleon is an animal that changes its colour every time. It has the ability to change to any particular colour of its present environment.

This animal does not easily become green or red just because it passes through any of these colours. For it to assume any particular colour, it has to stay under that particular colour for a considerable time and duration.

In other words, though the chameleon can change its colour, the change is tied to the amount of time it stays for its skin to absorb the colour of its prevailing environment. That is to say, the longer it stays under any colour, the more its skin absorbs the colour. This same principle applies to the things of the spirit. No person ever encounters dramatic and lasting changes if the fellow does not stay close to God enough.

The reason for shallow spirituality these days is the absence of quality time in the presence of the Lord. When preachers and their congregation are running around so many things, the outcome is shallow Christianity

We are transformed into the image and character of Christ when we stay close enough in communion with the Holy Spirit, who in turn impacts the life of God to us.

So if you need a change badly enough, then get into the presence of God and you will be amazed at the results that follow His presence.

CHAPTER 4
THE SOOTHING BALM

For if ye forgive men their trespasses, your heavenly Father will also forgive you. But if ye forgive not men their trespasses, neither will your Father forgive your trespasses.

(Matthew 6:14-15)

An exciting thing happened during the early Ministry of our Lord Jesus Christ. The fifth chapter of Matthew's Gospel says that the multitudes had been drawn to His ministry.

On seeing them, He climbed to a mountain (probably a higher platform which He used as a pulpit) to address them. After delivering what I may call "the Christian code of conduct" or what in theological circles is called the Beatitudes, the Disciples quickly got interested in the finer details of the long sermon.

Now with greater insight into the **ways** and **means** of conducting their lives, as opposed to the hypocritical ways of the Pharisees, they brought their most important area of concern to the Lord: **Teach us how to pray!**

I believe Jesus must have been thrilled at their request. Jesus was aware that the Disciples knew how to pray as Judaizers, but not as Christians. Every Jew is taught from the cradle to love and to worship God. However, the means of getting and securing the attention of God was what was lacking in their prayer.

A lot of people today have only a mental knowledge of God without a revelation -like kind of relationship. Such people's prayer becomes a ritual and a burden, instead of sweet communion with the Father.

What a tragedy today that people spend millions of hours the world over, praying to sticks, rocks, animals and demons - to secure divine intervention! God Almighty has always known that people will cry out to Him to be taught how to pray.

For the Disciples of Jesus, it was no longer a surprise that they sought for a prayer pattern that would deepen their communion with

God. After telling them the ABC of prayer, He (Jesus) gave them the password that opens and secures divine attention to all prayers - **forgiveness!**

Jesus simply told them "forgive and be free, or don't forgive and be blocked". Releasing people to go free when they are in our traps; causes God to release us from divine punishment when we offend Him and ask for mercy. No prayer crosses the roof of the house where it is prayed if the man or woman praying has not satisfied the minimum condition of securing divine attention.

It is sad to note today that in many places (including our Churches) people still enjoy living in unforgiveness and expect the Lord to hear them, heal them and deliver them. Just like the electric current stops flowing when it is bridged, unforgiveness is a circuit - breaker. The anointing of God will be shut off from blessing people if they persist in unforgiveness.

I remember being invited to preach for a Pastor friend in their Church in 1995 during a special programme. After my message, I called for people to be healed and filled with the Holy Spirit.

After the healing prayers, I asked those desiring to be baptized in the Holy Ghost to come forth. Four fellows stood up and walked to the platform. I laid my hands upon them all and thanked the Lord for the gift of the Holy Spirit upon their lives.

As I watched them, three of them spoke in tongues one couldn't speak. I placed my hand upon the last lady a second time, the Spirit of the Lord told me that the lady was living in enmity with another Christian girl in that Church. I asked her to stay aside while I prayed my last prayer.

After the service, I called the attention of the Pastor, to look into the life of the sister. Later, I discovered from their Pastor that the two ladies were living together in the same room, yet they were enemies! It is impossible to have the Devil and the Holy Spirit at the same time, one must make a choice!

Recent researches in the field of medicine have shown that there is a relationship between bitterness, and some chronic diseases people suffer. Unfortunately, many people do not know the source of their ailments except the old worn out excuse that the devil is troubling them. Actually, some sicknesses are self induced!

Some people believe that the bitterer they are against people, the more they would convey their feelings (message) clearer. Friend, don't live in bitterness, live for *betterness!* Ordinary anger can induce headache and dizziness if not properly arrested. Unforgiveness is a sign of spiritual immaturity.

It is therefore cheering news that the great Apostle Paul, who by all accounts in the Bible was the most hurt and maltreated Christian, has given us the secret of maintaining peace in all situations.

Put on therefore, as the elect of God, holy and beloved, bowels of mercies, kindness, humbleness of mind, meekness, long suffering; for bearing one another and forgiving one another, if any man have quarrel against any: And above all these things put on charity, which is the bond of perfectness. And let the peace of God rule in your hearts, to the which also ye are called in one body, and be ye thankful. (Colossians 3:12-15)

If we can learn to forbear, then we can forgive, and when we forgive the peace of God then rules in our hearts. This is the soothing balm.

May be today, you are carrying a deep burden in your heart which has weighed you down considerably.

You have tried on your own to handle the situation to no avail? Something has to be done practically in your situation and this simple.

You can apply these Scriptures in your life. His promise is that if you will allow love, which is the bond of perfectness to rule in your life, you will be released from all your burdens and sorrow.

Do it now and let God take the praise and glory in Jesus name.

CHAPTER 5

THE POWER OF ATTORNEY

There is tremendous power in words. When uttered, this power is released to act: either to create or destroy. For a Christian who has received and believed the Word of God, when he or she opens the mouth to speak, creative forces are unleashed into the environment to accomplish the purpose for which the words were uttered.

Like an un-exploded bullet, as long as it has not been fired, anybody can handle it. One can even put it inside the mouth without feeling any hurt.

But wait: that same bullet can shatter and blow one into pieces as soon as a gun has fired it. Things do not change unless words have been uttered either negatively or positively.

For verily I say unto you, that whosoever shall say unto this mountain, be thou removed, and be thou cast into the sea; and shall not doubt in his heart, but shall believe that those things which he saith shall come to pass; he shall have whatsoever he saith. (Mark 11:23)

If the mountain does not receive any command to move, it stays. Conversely, if the mountain hears the word `move', it has to obey because the force of the spoken word compels it to act accordingly.

Recently, I visited a dear friend of mine. On sighting me, he ran out and welcomed me in our usual way. After the initial pleasantries, he exclaimed, "I am all ears". He was simply saying. I am waiting to hear you talk about things around you because I am interested.

Have you ever attended a programme where they used a faulty Public Address System (PAS), and you find yourself straining your ears to hear what the speaker was saying? Perhaps, unable to grasp what was happening, you turned to a neighbour and asked, "What was he saying?

Well, this situation may not be a daily occurrence, but nonetheless, people across all races acknowledge the fact that thoughts are better communicated to others through words than facial expressions and gesticulations.

In Jesus' statement according to the book of Mark chapter 11, the emphasis of verse twenty-three is **"what you say or speak out".** It is amazing to discover the tremendous power that the ordinary mouth we have possesses.

In this book we have been sharing on peace. By way of decision, I would like to believe that you are desirous of possessing the power of peace and operating therein. Remember that some people already have taken this decision and they are better off with it, because there is no alternative to peace.

Operating in peace is not a fanciful past time. It is not achieved by simply saying that I wish I had peace like Mr X or Lady Y. This state is created by a decision to speak, and only speak sound words - the Words of God. Then and only then is the power to enjoy peace released to you.

Our mouths give expression to our thoughts, desires and plans. Actually, the things in our hearts are revealed through our vocal expressions. That is why in several places in the Bible, we are warned to be careful with what we say (James 3:1-2). The reason is simple: all things on earth are governed by words!

Through faith we understand that the worlds were framed by the word of God, so that things which are seen were not made of things which do appear. (Hebrews 11:3)

All agreements or misunderstandings are functions of words that have been uttered either positively or negatively. Now someone may be asking the question: can I ever have peace? The answer is perfectly yes, you can!

You have a right to live in peace, operate in peace - at the office, family, Church or village. However, the price of having peace is dependent on what you say or choose to say from henceforth.

Most tensions and anxieties are engineered by words. Our words go to a large extent in winning us friends or foes. Most hands that are strong enough to beat, slap, kick, chase or even punch people are incapable of action, unless they are commanded by words!

Conversely, most arms are laid down and even archenemies become best of friends when words are also uttered. Whichever side of the divide we find ourselves, we are primarily a product of the words we hear.

A soft answer turneth away wrath: but grievous words stir up anger (Proverbs 15:1).

I have come across some people in counselling sessions who sincerely want to know how to have and maintain peace in their houses, families and work places. Actually there is no magic wand for peace, except when Jesus Christ, the Prince of Peace has been invited and accepted.

When couples and entire families begin to pattern and order their lives, according to the Word of God, when the Spirit of God is allowed to control our lives, we become connected to the source of peace. You need connection to God to bring about a correction.

The fruit of the Spirit is peace (Galatians 5:22). Having the Spirit of God opens the door for the possessor to harvest the fruit of the Spirit - love, peace gentleness, meekness, long- suffering etc.

Any Spirit- filled person has a right to operate in peace when he or she is prepared to be careful in what he or she says.

Pleasant words are words of salvation and healing. Here is wisdom: What you say today may be the word, upon which someone's destiny may be decided tomorrow, so be in control of your speech.

I once read a pamphlet about a couple that had been quarrelling. They had tried to make peace among themselves to no avail. Confused and tired, they decided to seek for solution through a Marriage Counsellor. On the appointed day, the two walked into the counsellors' office like cat and dog. The counsellor asked them to tell their story.

From a vantage point, he quickly observed that their problem was "I must reply him/her syndrome". When they both "proved" their points, the man gave them separate appointments. The man went first, then the woman.

Curiously, on the day the woman visited, the counsellor brought a fine piece of granite. As usual, the woman narrated how the husband had been maltreating her. As she eagerly awaited the counsellor's final suggestions, she was amazed at how he handed her the sparkling granite. He simply told the woman, "Whenever you hear him speak again, put this object in your mouth and watch him". Surprised, the woman left for her house.

In the evening the husband came home, hollered as usual and began to talk carelessly. The woman quickly reached out for her piece of granite, put it into her mouth and watched the man. Embarrassed, the man stopped talking and went into his room. After some days of repeating this exercise, their problem was discovered.

The woman found out that the basis of quarrelling was that she replied to every attack. As she learnt to keep quiet, the man equally stopped his nagging business, so peace was at least restored. Later, they went back to the Counsellor, this time around holding hands together, telling him that the "magic" had worked.

They then resolved not to use offensive or foul language on each other. Remember you can win an argument for a season, but you cannot win peace by your deep desire to prove a point.

Many marriage partners have proved their points and also won convincing arguments. But at a cost! They lost the foundation of the union. It is like cutting one's nose to spite the face. In the end, the loser is the face.

The woman in our story stopped proving her point, and consequently won the elusive peace at home. You too can start from somewhere, and enjoy the right to peace in the midst of the storms around your life.

THE POWER OF CONFESSION

Confession is a medium of releasing divine power that is embedded in the Word of God. It is the art of repeating the Word of God with our mouths to create the desired results. Often so many folks think of confession in terms of confession of sins or atrocities one has committed.

In certain religious groups, thousands of faithful go on Weekends to tell the Priest their sins and expect his pronouncements to mitigate the effects of their sins.

The truth is that this kind of "confession" does not release the benefit of the Word of God to the confessors. They have the feeling of appearing before a Priest, but no assurance that their sins are either forgiven or forgotten.

However, there is a Bible kind of confession that involves taking the Word of God back to God on one hand, and also literally standing on the written Word to bring about a change in one's circumstances, or situations.

Take with you words and turn to the Lord: say unto him, take away all iniquity, and receive us graciously: so we will render the calves of our lips. (Hosea 14:2)

Your ability to take the right words to the Lord, determines your power to effect changes. Many who face challenges at home, office and careers, simply stand akimbo, watching the enemy deprive and disposes them of their inheritance?

Don't hold your hands crying over your situation. Rise up and speak what you want into existence. Don't confirm your doubts and fears; rather speak the solution in the midst of contrary evidence. That is how to bring every situation under your control.

One great truth about our confession is that it determines our possession. So your uttering power increases or reduces your having power. God confirmed this principle when He was dealing with the children of Israel.

Say unto them, as truly as I live, saith the Lord, as ye have spoken in my ears, so I will do unto you. (Numbers 14:28)

God Almighty told Moses to warn the children of Israel that what He heard them speak into His ears is exactly what He would carry out on their behalf. The children of Israel were passing through terrible times in the wilderness. Many complained, murmured and rebelled against God in their speech. They needed a reminder that their destiny lied in what they said.

Death and life are in the power of the Tongue: and they that love it shall eat the fruit thereof (Proverbs 18:21)

The fruit of death and life are already in everyone's mouth. Some people may not believe that there is the fruit of death in their mouth. Well, to check yourself, if you find this organ called tongue in your mouth, then you can be sure that this fruit is there. But wait a minute; neither the fruit of life nor of death has any force to cause any benefit or destruction unless someone has uttered a word!

CONFESSIONS THAT RELEASE POWER

Now join me to explore the riches of His grace available to us as we confess aloud these Scriptures. They surely carry powerful forces of peace that will enable anyone dominate fear and operate in peace.

Word: *I am the offspring of the Prince of peace (Isaiah 9:7)*

Confession: I confess that I have a root. I have my source in   Christ Jesus. I have the ability, grace and wisdom of God. Therefore, I am not a failure and would never be one, because my foundation is solid and secure.

Word: *The Lord lift up his countenance upon thee and give thee peace. (Numbers 6:26)*

Confession: The face of the Almighty God is lifted in my favour. The light of heaven is right now, shinning upon all dark areas of my life, giving me solutions and victory.

His peace is right now flooding my spirit, my heart and all around my environment.

Word: *Depart from evil, and do good; seek peace and pursue it (Psalms 34:14)*

Confession: Right now, my mind is departing from all evil intentions. I have the love of God in my heart. I have embraced peace, and I'm pursuing peaceful ways.

My heart is filled with good thoughts and I'm extending them to others. I refuse the spirit of revenge. I will not retaliate. I can forgive anyone. God is helping me to do so, even now.

Word: *Thou will keep him in perfect peace, whose mind is stayed on thee: because he trusteth in thee (Isaiah 26:3)*

Confession: God is keeping me in perfect peace. I refuse to worry and fret over anything. My trust is on the Lord. All my fears are over. I'm a completely new person on the inside. I praise God for a new day and fresh grace.

I will never be hunted by the mistakes of yesterday. My past is gone forever.

Word: *O that thou hadst hearkened to my commandments! Then had thy peace been as a river, and thy righteousness as the waves of the sea (Isaiah 48:18)*

Confession: I choose to obey the Word and not my feelings. Therefore my peace is like a river that is overflowing with joy and gladness. Praise God I have become unstoppable.

Word: *And when you come into an house, salute it. And if the house be worthy, let your peace come upon it: but if it be not worthy, let your peace return to you.*
(Matthew 10:12-13)

Confession: I confess that my heart, family and my entire household are worthy of God's peace. We welcome the spirit of peace right now in Jesus name! Glory to God, the Devil is already chased away.

Word: *Therefore being justified by faith, we have peace with God through our Lord Jesus Christ. (Romans 5:1)*

Confession: Jesus is my Saviour, Redeemer and Restorer of my life. I have been delivered from the powers of darkness, and translated into the kingdom of God's Son Jesus Christ.He is right inside of me, working out God's righteousness and character. I have been justified by faith and I know I now have peace with God. I refuse to fear again because I know I am already free.

Word: *And the LORD said unto him, Peace be unto thee; fear not: thou shalt not die. (Judges 6:23)*

Confession: I reject the spirit of fear, doubt and unbelief. I shall not die but live to declare the goodness of God in the land of the living.

I recover from today every ground I have lost through pride and haughtiness. I confess that from now my life shall be a perfect example of what the grace of God can do.

Word: *He hath delivered my soul in peace From the battle that was against me: for there weremany with me. (Psalms 55:18)*

Confession: I praise God that I am standing on the side of victory through the blood of Christ Jesus. All the battles of my life have ended in victory on my side. The power of God on my side will protect, preserve and keep me from all harm and evil. Glory is to God for His mighty power and grace upon my life.

Word: *When a man's ways please the LORD, he maketh even his enemies to be at peace with him. (Proverbs 16:7)*

Confession: The grace of the Lord is upon my marriage, business and career. I am a blessed and favoured person. The mark of peace is upon my life and destiny.

No man or woman can successfully hate me. My presence generates peace and the force of peace upon my life compels all who hate me to love me.

Word: *For thou shalt be in league with the stones of the field: and the beasts of the field shall be at peace with thee.(Job 5:23)*

Confession: I confess that the land and environment where I dwell shall not swallow me or oppress me. I have a covenant with all the sands, stones and grass of this environment.

I shall not be a victim of environmental forces. I have a portion of peace and goodness in this land. I shall surely not be moved.

I shall not be a victim of oppression and cruelty in the land where I live. By the special grace of God, I shall neither stumble nor fall at the hands of my enemies. Every power in this land where I live shall defend me.

I shall be in league with the stones of the field. This is my covenant portion today and forever.

On a personal note, you are required to speak out loud, or vocalise these confessions for them to have meaningful impact on your life. Merely reading these texts without open confession of the Scriptures on peace will remain ordinary statements of facts without them affecting you.

Dearly beloved, if you have said these Scriptures aloud to yourself in the morning, afternoon and evening, I guarantee you that you will be on your way to that life that is peace-filled. Expect God's reward system to work in your favour.

CHAPTER 6

TIME TO CROSS OVER

Many people are seeking for relevance in the scheme of things. Every facet of life is fully involved. From the political, economic, and social aspects of life to the military spheres, no area is exempted.

Across the nations, the echo has been, "I want to belong". The search for relevance and identity has been as old as the quest for survival upon the planet earth.

From the primitive days of man's existence on earth, to the days of the empires (Babylonian Empire, Medes/Persian Empire, Greek Empire, and of course the Roman Empire), man has been searching for distinct identity.

The disintegration of the Roman Empire, and the attendant balkanisation of the component units into the present European

Union, is a testimony to the fact that through the ages, the nations and peoples of the world are in search of relevance.

In the last six centuries, many nations of the world, especially the Europeans have embarked on discoveries of new lands and creation of new spheres of influence.

The competition to dominate and extend the frontiers of control has led to the historic "Scramble for Africa" and other parts of the world. The resultant effect of the scramble for Africa is the partitioning of the nations along language and political lines.

Today, we have the Anglophone group, the Francophone group, and the Dutch group, among others. These political groups represent the identities of the British, French and the Dutch.

From the historical perspective, we have deduced the fact that man wants to belong to a group, and therefore makes effort to be attached to others.

In modern times, with the democratic revolution, politicians canvass for voters to belong to their camps, as against those of their opponents.

The bottom line of all man's activities on earth today is to carve an identity for himself.

In the city of Bethlehem Judaea, many years ago, a man, whose name is Jesus Christ, was born. By the circumstance of His birth, He was definitely a *special child*. Angels heralded His birth, and they appeared to the least qualified group of people called shepherds.

To make the whole world know that a unique child has been born, God Almighty caused one star to outshine the others, and to actually stand out to guide certain people called" the wise men from the east", to the place where the child was kept.

By this announcement, the king of Judaea called Herod took particular notice of this unusual baby boy. Not prepared to take chances, he ordered all the male children from the ages of two years down to be killed - just because of one little boy called Jesus!

By God's divine providence, Jesus was preserved until Herod died. This son of Joseph the Carpenter, grew up in His father's house, and was trained in the father's craft. He was an obedient child in the house when He was growing up.

You will remember that God Almighty specifically told the angel that announced the details of Jesus' birth on earth, what He was born to be.

Now the birth of Jesus Christ was on this wise: When as his mother Mary was espoused to Joseph, before they came together, she was found with child of the Holy Ghost ... And she shall bring forth a Son, and thou shalt call his name Jesus: For he shall save his people from their sins (Matthew 1:18,21).

Jesus came for one purpose - to save His people from their sins. Now note the word *His people.* His mission was, and has always been, to save His people.

Though Jesus' conception was by the power of the Holy Ghost, yet He identified with mankind so that in the eyes of God, everyone on earth today is potentially "His people", if they meet the conditions laid down by God.

When Jesus was thirty years old, He began to manifest the purpose why God sent Him to the earth. He went first of all for baptism by John the Baptist, who incidentally was His forerunner. Before then, John had been calling people to repentance and confession of sins as he baptized them in the River Jordan.

So, to fulfil all righteousness, Jesus submitted to be baptized by John, though He had no sin to be repented of.

As Jesus was going to John for baptism, there were many people who witnessed it. The Bible clearly and pointedly tells us the divine purpose of God for allowing Jesus to be so publicly baptized.

And Jesus, when he was baptized, went up straightway out of the water: and lo, the heavens were opened unto him, and he saw the spirit of God descending like a dove, and lighting upon him: And lo, a Voice from heaven saying this is my beloved Son in whom I am well pleased. (Matthew 3:16-17)

Now, God has announced to all people that Jesus Christ is His Son, in whom He (God Almighty) is well pleased. God had set the ball rolling. The ministry of Jesus Christ is designed, approved and sanctioned by the Almighty God Himself.

All Judaea, Palestine, and indeed, the surrounding countries heard the divine message: **Jesus Christ is the Saviour of the world- Hallelujah!** Now with divine back up, Jesus began His ministry of destroying every work of the Devil in the lives of men and women.

Literarily, thousands were healed, delivered, saved, encouraged and empowered.

As the name and fame of Jesus was spreading across the land and coasts of Palestine, so was His follower ship. People had to make a choice - to follow Him, ignore, or reject Him.

As Jesus kept healing, and changing lives; many people from different professions in life began to choose Him. Certain fishermen, Customs' officials, others who were tired of empty religion, abandoned all their trades to become full-time Disciples.

Obviously, for these people, their lives had deep needs, which could not be satisfied by any other person except Jesus Christ. It was during this time of spiritual awakening among the populace that a notable religious leader felt a deep need in his soul, which must be satisfied.

Having been brainwashed by the religious leaders of the day that Jesus was not worth following, this man whose name is Nicodemus (a Greek name which means literarily-conqueror of the people) - a notable Pharisee decided to visit Jesus Christ.

However, due to his position in the religious hierarchy (as some people are today), he decided to go by night.

Here is a man, who outwardly was reputed to be a religious man, yet he was not sure of the position of his soul - whether he would end up in hell fire, or in heaven.

The same problem Nicodemus had is what is holding millions of people from having a saving faith in the Lord Jesus Christ. Religious titles and other man-made schemes have stood as a barrier between men and God. People have stopped having encounters with God directly, but prefer to run around religious orders that are vain.

For Nicodemus, going to Jesus by night was the ideal thing, as official religious set-up did not permit him to fraternise with Jesus Christ. Thank God, he however made it by night. Any time one meets Jesus Christ it is still acceptable.

Now let us capture the encounter as recorded in the Bible.

There was a man of the Pharisees, named Nicodemus, a ruler of the Jews: The same came to Jesus by night, and said unto him, Rabbi, we know

that thou art a teacher come from God: we know that no man can do these miracles that thou doest, except God be with him. Jesus answered and said unto him, verily, verily, I say unto thee, Except a man be born again, he cannot see the kingdom of God (John 3:1-3).

Here is one of the most glorious words that came out of the mouth of Jesus. For Nicodemus, he came to enquire about Jesus. He started by acknowledging that Jesus came from God. The natural thing for Jesus to do was to appreciate the beautiful compliments of Nicodemus.

But Jesus cut him short by His reply. Jesus told Nicodemus that **mere knowledge about God, and what He can do is not enough**. How good God is, is not enough, but what is needful is the all-important question Jesus threw back to Nicodemus. **Except a man be born again, he cannot see the Kingdom of God (John 3:3).**

Friend, as you are reading this book, **are you born again?** Don't tell me you go to your Church regularly, take Holy Communion and have religious titles, so was Nicodemus. Maybe you are saying, I love God - so was Nicodemus: he was a Pharisee!

According to Jesus, merely knowing God and being religious does not guarantee entrance into the Kingdom of God. What gives the key of entrance is this simple word: **You must be born again.** Yes, you must do it because it is necessary for your soul to enter heaven.

It is time for you to move from religion to Christ. The world is not lacking religious people, but is certainly looking for genuine Christians. You must come out, stand out and be counted. For a long time, people have been gravitating between religion and Christ.

It is costly at this time to be neutral. Soon the heavenly bell will ring, and the trumpet of God will sound, and there surely shall be a verdict.

And I saw a great white throne, and him that sat on it, from whose face the earth and the heaven fled away, and there was found no place for them. And I saw the dead, small and great, stand before God; and the books were opened: and another book was opened, Which is the book of life: and the dead were judged out of those things written in the books, according to their works....And whosoever was not found written in the book of life was cast into the lake of fire.
(Revelation 20; 11-12, 15-emphasis mine).

The verdict is that whosoever has not pitched his camp, and identified with Jesus Christ **now,** shall soon end up in hell fire. Friend, do everything possible to get your name registered in this book of life. It is time to cross over to Jesus.

And after this (the death of Jesus) Joseph of Arimathaea, being a disciple of Jesus, <u>but secretly for fear of the Jews</u>, besought Pilate that he might take away the body of Jesus: and Pilate gave him leave. He came therefore and took the body of Jesus. And there came also Nicodemus, which at the first came to Jesus by night, and brought a mixture of myrrh and aloes... Then they (Joseph, Nicodemus and co.) took the body of Jesus.... to bury. (John 19: 38-40: emphasis mine).

One major theme that runs throughout the pages of the Bible is the fact that time on earth is highly limited. In other words, nothing on earth including human beings has limitless time to function and finish all that one is destined to accomplish.

The brief nature of life on earth has made it imperative for everyone to order one's life so as to live purposefully and meaningfully.

However, despite the desirability of ordered life, not many people eventually exercise the discretion of doing the right things at the right time. Indeed, majority of the people would rather prefer to do the right thing at the wrong time.

Our Scripture reference identifies two men: Joseph of Arimathaea and Nicodemus as two key figures who were present during the life and Ministry of the Lord Jesus. These two men took the right decision at the wrong time.

Joseph of Arimathaea was a Disciple of the Lord Jesus, but secretly because he feared losing the friendship of the Jews. He preferred to trade off his relationship with Jesus on the altar of social connections and the like. All the days of his life, he was carrying a burden of secret admiration without open identification.

Nicodemus on the other hand feared losing his 'ecclesiastical' seat and position among the religious people than to identify with Christ openly. When the Jews had finally killed the Lord Jesus, they came out boldly to the Governor Pilate, to identify with a 'dead' Jesus.

Before they came, the cat was already out of the bag. It was like medicine after death.

They were not useful to Jesus in life and showed up when there was no need for their ministry.

One fact that has emerged as we are approaching the end of all things is that the world will always try to kill what it cannot control.

There are many Christians that are taking decisions to pray, study the Word, attend fellowship with fellow believers, give to support the work of evangelism and witness for Christ: - all at the wrong time!

These people lose divine opportunities heaven has granted them by wasting such times on the wrong things.

As you are reading this book, do you know that you have another chance to show love to your wife, help the needy around you; speak that tender word your spouse has been eagerly awaiting to hear, organise your life to fall in line with God's will for your life?

Do you know that a good seed you sow at the right time could dramatically alter the course of someone's life on earth?

The story of Nicodemus and his friend shows that we have a limited time here on earth to do what we know to be good.

Fear prevented them from identifying with Jesus openly. When they finally showed up, they were only involved in the ministry of burying what they ought to have prevented from dying.

As you serve God this year, may nothing hinder you from showing up and following through to the end? Remember you have another chance today to do something around your environment and change someone's life for good. Use this fresh opportunity rightly.

Joseph of Arimathaea and Nicodemus served Jesus in death. They waited until He died before identifying with Him. Now that you are alive, won't you serve him while you are still breathing? Are you among those who continually give one excuse or the other?

Many able and capable men and women are not involved today in the right kind of ministry God has ordained for them because of posts and positions that the religious hierarchy has given them. They prefer to save their names and self respect than to defend the cause of Christ in their lives. Are you still a Nicodemus or have your eyes been opened to the current realities?

It is time for you to show up on the side of Jesus. If you have not done it before now, bow down your knees, and call upon the name of the Lord. Do not wait to find the opinion of your friends, relations or even associates.

The demand is urgent and the necessity is compelling. It would be disastrous to postpone this epic encounter. All your life depends on what you do now with Jesus Christ.

The dark curtain is falling upon this earth and the hearts of men are already failing them. Turn aside and set your life in order.

The salvation train is at your doorstep. You have been hanging around for long. It is time to jump in and be seated. Say yes to that inner conviction and be free indeed. Do it now, so that the Lord will take the glory.

CHAPTER 7

THE SECRET OF REST

Every successful venture in life is anchored on certain secrets, which the failure never had access to. God Almighty has a secret for keeping the universe in shape. Jesus Christ had a secret for His awesome power that accompanied His earthly ministry.

Even now, the Holy Spirit has a secret that enables Him to convict a sinner of his sins, and cause a righteous transformation in the lives of the most horrible criminals.

You may be asking the question: how did Jesus Christ, and indeed His most outstanding spokesman the Apostle Paul, enjoy the fullness of peace, in spite of much opposition and hostilities?

The Bible clearly told us that they lived surrendered lives to the purpose and Will of God (See John 5:30, 2 Tim 1:12).

You too can learn, and master the secret of rest from all storms.

Now, if you are ready, let us consider the foundations upon which restful lives are built. In other words, if you are seeking for peace and rest in your own life, here are the things you must know and practise.

<u>Obey the first Commandment.</u> One of the deepest mysteries God Almighty has instituted on earth today is the marriage Institution, and the attendant family tree. Every man, woman, boy or girl that walks on earth is rooted in a family. No person came to this earth without that family channel.

Basically, the family begins with the man and the woman who are called the husband and the wife. The offspring of their relationship constitute the children. So, every child has a source from where his or her life started. This source carries powerful influence and authority over the destiny of children born to that home.

Every family has her family blessings as well as the family curse. These two powerful forces are always transferred from parents to children. Children that merit the blessing, through their attitudes have different outcomes in their lives on earth. Those who merit the curses, through their actions also have different lives on earth.

The implication is that, how a person lives on earth is primarily influenced by the clear choices one has made in relation to the family. The family connection is so important that God Almighty gave a commandment as to how one should relate with the father and the mother.

Children, obey your parents in the Lord: for this is right. Honour thy father and mother; (which is the first commandment with promise;) That it may be well with thee, and thou mayest live long on the earth. (Ephesians 6: 1-3)

The key to blessings, peace and rest is clearly stated in that Scripture above: 'honour your father and your mother'. Honouring one's biological parents is the pathway to a life of rest. It also positions one to enjoy long life on earth.

There are people today who have their life of misery and restlessness rooted in the way and manner they have treated their parents. Despising, neglecting and abandoning of one's parents are a source of curse, which could only be remedied by making amends.

If you are reading this book now and you are not at peace with your parents, no amount of prayer and confession would change your condition.

If you are living in the city, and enjoying all the good things of life, while your father or mother are in the village barely surviving, how do you think that the hamburger in your mouth would taste so sweet?

If you beat up your parents for whatever reason, abuse and speak ill of them privately, or publicly, the curse of the Lord is upon your life. You must make restitution for God to forgive you of the sacrilege.

Don't confess peace, peace, when you have troubled your source. When your behaviour causes your parents to sigh, and mourn, you are indirectly troubling your own soul. Don't uncover your parent's nakedness and expect your own life to be covered.

Every wrong thing you do against your parents will fly on your face and fight you until you are vexed on every side. So rise up today and honour your parents, so that it may go well with you on the face of the earth.

On a personal note, you must know that there is a difference between honouring your parents and obeying them. You may not always obey your parents in everything (especially when what they are asking you to do is against the written Word of God).

However, you have a commandment to honour them even when you do not agree totally with them. In other words, you can disagree without being disagreeable. This involves a measure of divine understanding and wisdom in relationships.

<u>Don't live in strife:</u> One of the easiest things to do on earth today is to have one's pound of flesh. For one to extract this pound, one must equally be under the powerful spirit called strife.

Strife is simply the spirit of quarrelling and bickering in order to have a better advantage over others. One of the most classic examples of the manifestation of this spirit is recorded in the thirteenth chapter of the book of Genesis.

And Lot also, which went with Abram, had flocks, and herds and tents. And the land was not able to bear them that they might dwell together: for their substance was great, so that they could not dwell

together. And there was strife between the herdmen of Abram's cattle and the herdmen of Lot's cattle: and the Cananite and the Perizzite dwelled then in the land. And Abram said unto Lot, let there be no strife, I pray thee, between me and thee, and between my herdmen and the herdmen; for we be brethren. Is not the whole land before thee? Separate thyself, I pray thee, from me:if thou will take the left hand, then I will go to the right, or if thou depart to the right hand, then I will go to the left. And Lot lifted up his eyes, and beheld all the plain of Jordan, that it was well watered everywhere.... Then Lot choose him all the plain of Jordan, and Lot journeyed east: and they separated themselves the one from the other. Abram dwelled in the land of Canaan, and Lot dwelled in the cities of the plain, and pitched his tent toward Sodom (Genesis 13:5-12).

Here, Abram being the matured and less selfish man called his young nephew, and pointedly told him that it was not good for them to strive for the land.

Here, Lot's self-centredness came to the fore, when he "chose him all the plain of Jordan". It would be recalled that the man God gave the entire land was Abram.

Lot, who was just a dependant to Abram decided to have all the plain of Jordan.

This obviously was the most fertile soil in the entire region. Abram was left to pick the crumbs and the not-too-attractive land.

However, the sovereignty of God and His divine reward system turned Abram's waste land into one that flows with milk and honey, Not only was Abram compensated for his principled stand, God equally decreed that the land he had be his; and that of his descendants forever.

As for Lot, (whose name means covering) he intended to expand his empire by pitching his tent **towards** Sodom. Think about it: the direction of a man determines where he would end up. Lot thought that moving towards Sodom (which literarily means burning) was a harmless exercise.

But how he found himself **actually in** Sodom is what we may not explain here. His covetous choice led him to destruction to the extent that he left Sodom without a single pin!

All greedy and subversive people will end up one day bruising their lives. No one can beat God's justice system any day. Abram won without fighting, believing that God would be in a better position to handle all matters.

If you don't strive, you won't strike. The best way to lose divine support is to engage in an unnecessary striving after things. God says, "Vengeance is mine, I will repay"(Romans 12:19). Whoever God fights for will surely have a victory that outlasts all other things.

Walk in love: The freest person on earth is the one that operates by love. As I was writing this section, I got a report of a young man in Ministry who undermined the position of his Senior Pastor.

Unknown to the older Minister, the young man passed across to the Headquarters of the Church, malicious reports that were intended to cause disaffection between the elder Minister and National leadership.

God miraculously worked in such a way that before the evil plans could be perfected, the younger Minister fell into immorality and had to quit the Ministry unceremoniously.

Wherefore let him that thinketh he standeth take heed lest he fall (1 Corinthians 10:12).

One of the most callous things happening on earth today is the spirit of betrayal: So many people handle the affairs of others without feelings.

Other people (especially among some Christians), feel that they have a permanent spot in the grace of God and can never be called to question one day by God Almighty.

The level of hardness of heart in relationships and associations has driven many to conclude, that the love of God is no longer real today on earth.
The Scriptures still insist that we should walk in love or be guided by love actions always.

Be ye therefore followers of God, dear children And walk in love, as Christ also hath loved us and hath given himself for us an offering and a sacrifice to God for a sweet smelling savour (Ephesians 5:1-2).

Love is the force that defeats all opponents. It is the hammer that breaks even the most stubborn hearts. It is weak in its operation, but very profound in its results.

Jesus Christ knew that Judas would betray Him and even told His followers so. Yet, He allowed Judas to eat with Him and take the communion bread and wine with the rest of the Disciples.

He watched Judas scheme for His betrayal and eventual crucifixion. Jesus did not fight back or changed His attitude towards Judas, even to the last hour! What was the result?

When Judas saw the power of love, he counted the thirty pieces of silver - the price at which he sold the Lord Jesus and returned the blood money. Unable to contain the grief over his betrayal, he eventually committed suicide!

Where is Judas today? Where is Jesus today? The difference is clear. Those who will make the difference in these last days are not men of fists, but men of love. The path of liberty is the path of love.

No matter what men may say or do, please cast your vote on living a life of love. This is the only lifestyle that appreciates and generates lasting dividends.

Be in the presence of God: One of the most striking experiences in life is to come in contact with the presence of God. When the Apostle John was banished to the Island of Patmos, he was not really perplexed about the environment he found himself.

From the beginning, the Disciples had been trained to endure hardship for the sake of the gospel. They faced great opposition and oppression from the religious leaders of their day.

Joy was the hallmark of those early Christians, even in the most adverse conditions.

As for anyone else, being in a dangerous and lonely Island could be damaging to a chicken-hearted fellow. But this was not the case with John. He knew how to create the presence of God. He gives us the secret of God's presence.

I John, who also am your brother, and companion in tribulation, and in the kingdom and patience of Jesus Christ, was in the Isle that is called Patmos, for the word of God, and for the testimony of Jesus Christ. I was in the spirit on the Lord's day..
(Revelation 1:9-10).

John says he was there for the Word of God. As John was banished for preaching and living the Word of God, he made time to be in the spirit. Being in the spirit does not mean that one becomes a ghost and begins to make shriek sounds. It simply means being Spirit- conscious.

This state of life is achieved when one finds time, (quality time) to meditate on the Word of God and prayer. On the day John was in the spirit, the presence of God came down tangibly to the extent that John bowed down to the glory and power of the Almighty. One thing the presence of God does is that it always brings reassurance to the believer. That is why David shouted in Psalms.

Thou wilt shew me the path of life: in thy presence is fullness of joy, at thy right hand there are pleasures for ever more (Psalms 16:11)

Yes, in the presence of God, there is fullness of joy. God is the author of joy. He has it without measure. Anyone who is able to create the environment wherein God can come into any situation automatically gains strength and courage.

And Nehemiah, which is the Tirshatha, and Ezra the priest the scribe, and the Levites that taught the people saith unto the people, this day is holy unto the Lord your God; mourn not, nor weep... go your way, eat the fat, drink the sweet, and send portions unto them for whom nothing is prepared. For this day is holy unto the Lord, neither be ye sorry; for the joy of the Lord is your strength (Nehemiah 8:9-10).

Friend, get excited in the Lord your God. Don't allow the Devil to weigh you down. You are on the track of success don't derail the train. The love of God for you is unique. You are the one God has been searching for.

Let go the works of the Devil and start getting excited in the things of God. God's hands are for you. His grace is released in your direction.

All the days of tension and intimidation from the hand of the Devil are over. There is a new dawn, an era of peace God has packaged for you through Jesus Christ. Receive this grace from God and expect your peace to abide.

Staying on the Word of God. Everything on earth and in heaven is a product of words that have been spoken. When God said, 'let there be light' the Word was said in the realm of the spirit, but its effects were noticed in the natural.

That is to say, that the Word of God can look ordinary, but its effects are extra-ordinary. Anyone who is looking for a turn-around must key in to the Word of God.

The story of David is a classic illustration of what the Word can do in the moulding of a person's destiny. After a series of troubles that beset the life of David on his way to the throne of Israel, he recommended to all who are troubled, a sure way of peace and prosperity.

Blessed is the man that walketh not in the counsel of the ungodly, nor standeth in the way of sinners, nor sitteth in the seat of the scornful. But his delight is in the law of the Lord; and in his law doth he meditate day and night. And he shall be like a tree planted by the rivers of water, that bringeth forth his fruit in his season; his leaf also shall not wither; and whatsoever he doeth shall prosper (Psalms 1: 1-3).

David realised that meditating on the Word could produce rest to any person who delighted in the Word. The Scripture says 'whatsoever he does prospers'.

Many would pay any price to have the ability control all things around them. This privilege comes only to those who will stay on the Word, no matter what they face in life.

There is a sure promise from God to you personally. Any force of hell cannot reverse it. Lay hold on it today and expect it to keep you at all times.

Now open your Scriptures to Second Thessalonians the third chapter.

Now the Lord of peace himself give you peace always by all means. The Lord be with you all. (2 Thessalonians 3:16)

This promise is for you. God will use every available means to ensure that your peace is guaranteed. Now the power of God has been released in your favour. Your days of woe are over. Your new sun has risen!

Expect a miracle of peace today!

If you have not made peace with Jesus Christ, and desire to have your name entered into the Lamb's Book of life, bow down your knees right now, and call upon the name of the Lord, and you shall be saved. Will you do it? Do it now and God bless you.

Let us pray:

Dear Father in heaven, I recognize that you are the only true God. I know I am a sinner and have fallen short of your glory. Forgive me of all my sins and iniquities.

I believe that Jesus is the Son of God, and that He died on the Cross of Calvary for my sins. I believe that He (Jesus) was raised from the dead for my justification. I now confess that Jesus Christ is my Lord and personal Saviour. Thank you Father for saving me, Amen.

Now that this book has blessed you, pick your pen and write me immediately.

My address is:
Alozie I. Ikonne
P. O. Box 6558
Aladinma P. O. (Postal code 460231)
Owerri- Nigeria
West Africa
Tel: +234-803-3438251
E-mail: fountainmedia@yahoo.com;
pastor@fgmin.org